Emma Saves Her Life

Emma Saves Her Life

Poems by Naton Leslie

Turning Point

Published by Turning Point
P.O. Box 541106
Cincinnati, OH 45254-1106

ISBN: 9781933456812
LCCN: 2007905339

Poetry Editor: Kevin Walzer
Business Editor: Lori Jareo

Cover design: Sergio Sericolo

Visit us on the web at www.turningpointbooks.com

Table of Contents

Acknowledgments

"Emma To Herself" first appeared in *Chachalaca Poetry Review* as "Emma Writes to Herself" and in a slightly different form, "Emma Can See Again" in *The Roanoke Review*, "Emma Hangs on to What She Can" and "Will Can't Eat but Emma Keeps Stocking up" in *Fresh Ground*, "From Emma's Scrapbook: 1921" in *West Branch* as "From Emma's Scrapbook," "From Emma's Scrapbook: 1998," "Emma Watches Other People Work," and "Emma Does What She Has to" in *Poem*, "From Emma's Scrapbook: 1953," and "From Emma's Scrapbook: 1949" in *The Comstock Review*, "From Emma's Scrapbook: 1929" in *The Patterson Literary Review*, "Will Feeds the Livestock" and "Emma Gets Nostalgic" in *Illuminations*, "Emma Complains about Will" and "Emma Gets Around" in *Cyphers*, "Emma Lists a Few Certainties" in *Kerf*, "From Emma's Scrapbook: 1938" and "Emma Waits out a Spring Snow" in *Pegasus*, "Emma Stays in the House" in *The Texas Review*, and "Emma Endures the Dirt Track" in *The Sow's Ear Poetry Review*. Thanks to David Baratier, Jonathan Blumberg, Rob Faivre, Elaine Handley and Pat Moran for their careful reading and advice. And a special thanks to Sue, who both edits and sustains me.

For all of my grandmothers.

Introduction

The woman known in these poems as Emma was based in large part on my paternal grandmother. Born in 1907, Emma Margaret Foster lived in the hills and hollows of western Pennsylvania, went to a one-room schoolhouse through the fifth grade, then married, and outlived, two men. What she experienced in her ninety-four years, in nearly the full length of the 20th century, was a transformation of culture perhaps unprecedented in history.

In some ways all of her life was taken up with saving. As a woman who was born and raised on a hardscrabble mountain farm, and who lived in direct connection with the land, Emma was always in the process of saving something. She saved the last of the green tomatoes to make relish; she saved geraniums from frost; she saved rags from which she made rugs. She was frugal, not as a virtue or out of necessity, but as a way-of-life. Much of her life was involved with the harvesting and processing of food, and these stores, kept in her root cellar, she called her *preserves*.

And then she saved some more. She saved stories by the dozens, and kept them alive by telling them to anyone who would listen, long, cascading strings of stories. She saved husbands from the dark days of the Great Depression and from disease, only to lose them anyway. Emma saved everyone who came within her prodigious power to preserve. Much of what I know about my family roots comes through her, in the things she told me. Through her I got to glimpse a way-of-life which was fading from view and memory, and now that I have grown old enough to see the world transformed beyond all recognition from the days of my youth, I understand some of the urgency she must have felt in wanting to save what she knew, to *have her say*, as she would have put it. Now I know why she put such stock in remembering things. Forgetting is all too easy.

A great deal of what she saved about life came out in her letters, and these letters are the basis of most of the poems in this book. For 15 years, when I was away at college pursing this degree or that, my grandmother wrote to me. I don't know if she wrote to anyone else—perhaps others in my family received letters, but no one has ever said so—but she wrote often to me because I would write back. My letters were breezy and light, covering health, family news, or the weather. Hers were much different, and much better.

Emma often wrote to me when she couldn't sleep. Whenever she woke in the middle of the night she would leave her bed, sit down at the little desk in the parlor, take out some stationary, write whatever was on her mind, and stuff it into an envelope addressed to me. In the morning she would put a stamp on it and set it out for the mail carrier. From what I could tell she never revised or reread what she wrote, nor referred to my letters, even to answer a question I might have asked.

During those years I was always delighted to get these letters, and often surprised by them as well; sometimes when I went to the mailbox, a pretty startling chunk of my grandmother's psychic landscape would come tumbling out. After all, the things which wake us in the middle of the night, and keep us awake, can be pretty disturbing and stark.

Often, she would think about things which were happening to her, but just as often she would mull over the past, revisiting memory. At other times one thought would seamlessly suggest another, or become one-and-the-same. The older Emma became, the more intertwined things grew in her mind. Her letters were a way for her to sort out these interconnections, and to explore their inseparable truths. In the poems which resulted from these letters, I edited out any sign of myself, preferring to treat the letters as diary entries. I have also tried to preserve the measure and tone of her voice, as her written voice distinctly echoed her spoken voice, one perfectly suited to her stories. Finally, I tried to preserve some sense of her failing health—she suffered from Alzheimer's Disease, and this was also increasingly evident in her letters. I've often wondered if she wrote things down in a last-ditch effort to keep her memories from eroding away.

When she turned ninety and had to live in a long-term care facility, my parents cleaned out her house, removing the most personal of her possessions. That was when they discovered that she had kept a scrapbook since the age of nine. They turned over the four-inch thick binder to me, and in it I found newspapers clippings, letters from her mother, photographs, cards and recipes—things preserved because they had some resonance, not merely because they might be useful. These became triggers to another sequence of poems, interior monologues in third-person point-of-view, which address this additional layer of saved things.

What I hope emerges is a poetic narrative which restores her voice and keeps her memories alive. Emma gets to have her say, finally, in a larger context. In truth, my grandmother disliked her first name, preferring to be called Margaret, but in renaming her Emma, I was able to make her into someone I didn't know, someone with whom I had to become acquainted anew through her letters and through the voice in the poems. Other names have been changed as well, simply to complete the fictive world in which I placed her, but everything else here is true, as it was told to me. I may have combined stories, altered others, but each bit of saving is an act of collaboration between what might be lost, and the rescuer. Here, finally, a hundred years after her birth, Emma speaks again, and through poetry, her life is made present to anyone who chooses to listen.

N.L.
Ballston Spa, NY
2007

Emma Readies for a Party

Got up early this morning,
couldn't stay in bed any longer
as my back bothers me.
Have to be up and ready.
Don't have to spend the day
cleaning as I have a lady
who does it for me now.
I'll be 78 on the 24th.

The PA Farmers Mutual is having
its banquet. My husband Will
helped start it when the farmers
figured they could get together
and rebuild what burned.
When the Ritter farm failed,
Will took their two hundred acres
of rock, and a dry herd.

Got a nice dress for the banquet.
I always dread it, but then I go
and have a good time—except
last year. Some of those bitches
from the big farms brought pies
—they didn't make them either.
Then one of them had nerve
enough to comment on my crust.
She had just had an operation
on a boil on her face, one eye
covered in a pirate patch.

Flat, she said, *No flake to it.*
I worked half the morning
on pies and bread and now

these fancy fannies were talking.
I wheeled around, lifted her
patch and smacked her right on
the boil. You should've seen
her go down. Will said later
I was a hard woman to take
anywhere. I just laughed.

From Emma's Scrapbook: 1916

Her grandmother dies in 1916,
so Emma starts a scrapbook
with the clipped obituary,
her first piece saved.
She is nine years old.

The newspaper lists things
about Lula which Emma never
knew: maiden name, *Foringer*,
born in Brady's Bend in 1830,
kin stretching out to Oklahoma,
survivors, the paper calls them.
The column names ten children,
which Emma memorizes
as though someday she might
need to call out to them.
Emma is mentioned only as one
of forty grandchildren.
Even at nine

she relishes this record,
this final recalling
and adding it all up.
Such little room given
to store the many facts
of one woman's long life,
and Emma wishes she had
known her this well
while she lived. She finds

a place in her Bible to tuck
the little slip. As a survivor
she knows she'll have more.

Emma Tells about Her Brothers

Now here's one I can finally tell.
My brother Samuel was called Jack
by most, Black Jack by some,
and at the time I thought
it was because he was dark-haired
like our Seneca grandmother,
he and baby brother Freddie,

who died in my arms
when I was fourteen,
though his hair might
have turned had he lived
long enough. We had taken
Freddie to town to see
Doc Kettler and he said
he was fine, just a little
colicky, and on the way back
up the mountain, halfway
up the long wooden steps,
he just quit breathing.
I didn't even know it
until I felt him loosen.
He was such a tight baby,

always ready to cry.
Jack used to play harmonica
for him at night when
he was breathing ragged.
He took Freddie's death hard.
I used to sing along
and the baby cooed.
Jack would call me *Songbird.*

When I was older and began
keeping company in the evenings,
something happened.
I've never been sure
about the whole story.
I was always afraid
to say anything. Now I can,
because Jack's dead.
His wife wrote me
he died just last week.

So this is what happened.
One evening I was coming home
and heard footsteps behind me
on the steps. The faster
I climbed, the faster they did

When I got in the house
only Jack was still up.
I was all out of breath,
and Jack asked:
What's fretting you?
So I told him. He smiled,
and I guessed he thought
I was a nervous Nellie.

After a week I was coming home
late again and I heard those
same footsteps—then a shot
cracked over the mountains
and I heard thuds as something
rolled down the steps. I flew
up to the house and about
broke through the door.
Jack came in right after.

I said, *Jack! Did you hear
that shot?* He sat down,
looked away from me,
and began cleaning a revolver
on the kitchen cutting board.
What shot? he said,
*What are you twittering about
Songbird?* He was as cool
as the night, and from that
point on I worried about him.

Well, not long after he left
the farm and we heard rumors.
I knew he was up to something,
but I didn't know what. All
I knew was he started driving
a new car, a Hudson sedan,
though times were pretty tough.

I asked mother about him,
why he never visited for long,
why he seemed to have so much
money, why he'd gotten this high
pitched laugh, why he sometimes

looked away, over his shoulder,
even when he was talking to you,
but she'd just purse her mouth
like she was eating something
bitter, and say nothing back.
That was just like mother.
She was either always worried
or never worried, you couldn't
tell. She'd just turn away

and shove her hands into cleaning
a chicken or dishes. There are
things mother knew what
went with her to the grave.

Jack got married to a gal
from down in Kittanning
by the name of Flossie McCleary,
one of the McClearys
from Lost Stocking Ridge.
I liked her. She was funny
and treated Jack good, never
called him Jack, always *My Samuel*.
She thought the world of him.

Jack settled down a bit,
had two kids, took a regular job.
For a while he mined coal
but a new ticket boss came up
from New Castle, and Jack
beat him near to death
for docking the workers.
Back then they held everything
against a miner's pay: broken
handles, dynamite caps, even
the soap they used at day's end.

This crooked boss would issue
bobtail checks—on payday
the charges would cancel out
the wages. They say it took
three men to pull Jack off,
but I can't say for sure
as all we got home were rumors.

Then I got married and we lived
down by the Mahoning River.
One morning Jack pulled up

our lane in that big Hudson.
I was hanging laundry
and ready to give him
the dickens for kicking up
all of that dust, but when
I saw his car was full
of bullet holes, the windows
mostly blown out, I felt
that old worry crawl my neck.

He said he had to go away.
*Tell Flossie and the kids
I'm dead—it's for the best.*
He gave me a new silver dollar
To remember me by.
That was 1926, the last
year they made them.
I still have it.

So the years went on
and there was no word,
not even rumors. Finally,
about sixty years later
—could it really be
that long--my sister
Olivia, who I never liked,
though that's all I want
to say about that right now,
heard he was living in Nevada.

So I called information,

got the exchanges and called
again until I found three Samuel
Wosters in Reno. I wrote them all:

Hello. My name was once Emma
Margaret Woster. Then I thought
for a bit and said, *My brother*
used to call me Songbird.
He was named Samuel Woster,
but they all used to call him
Black Jack. Are you my brother?

One wrote back and said yes.

So that's how I learned what
happened. I wonder if mother
knew, kept it to herself
right up to when she died,
only six years after he left.

Back then he was working
for the revenue agents,
going after moonshiners
by pretending to be one.
They had a name for it,
he said, they called it
Operating without shoes.
He hauled their liquor,
watched the stills
then turned them all in.

They caught on and he had to go
into hiding, so the feds sent him
out west. Those whiskey boys
were a bad bunch, and he worried

23

they'd go after Flossie
and the children, or even us.
Now he was remarried. He sent
me a photo of himself standing
in front of a new house
with a woman. He was retired
on a government pension,
and said he liked to garden
when I told him about mine,
but he complained that things
grew hard in Nevada.
And he begged me not to tell
Flossie or the children.
She never remarried because
I think she knew all along
that he wasn't really dead,
I did tell him that.

It's been too long, he wrote back.
Flossie was in a nursing home
and my nephew and niece lived
far off, so I never did tell
anyone until now. He said
he hoped we had all given up
on him. I reminded him that

back when Freddie was ill
we never gave up on him,
we'd give him songs to keep him
at peace, like *Turkey in the Straw,
Red River Valley*, or one song,
with a title I don't remember,
about some fellow who killed
his sweetheart, cut off her head
and dumped her in the Ohio River,

then was all tore up with grief.
Jack taught me all the words.

It was a high lonesome song,
so a girl's voice went good
on it. The mouth harp parts
were spooky and pained. I recall
thinking this is no kind of song
for a sick baby, but it was
one of Freddie's favorites,
put him to sleep every time.

Who would have figured that?
But that was Jack—he knew things,
more than what was good for him.

Emma Adds to Her Story

Two more things. First,
the reason they called
the place where Flossie's
people lived Lost Stocking Ridge
was because one time a peddler
came to Kittanning selling stockings
and other nice things for women.
He made his rounds, then asked
about a short-cut to Dubois
as he was behind schedule.
They sent him up the logging road,
what is now route 29, which goes
up around Hawthorn and Frogtown.

Well, he ran into a bunch of them
moonshiners up on the ridge.
They caught him and killed him,
I said they were bad news,
even worse when they were all
hopped up on hootch. They went
wild and threw his stockings
and such all over the mountainside.
They blew around up there
for weeks, and that's how
they knew the peddler was dead.
And that's why it was called that.

Second, my sister Olivia.
I didn't like her because
she was mean and lazy.
She thought she was prettier
than me and took a man
I was spending time with

just to prove it. She didn't
even like him, but she knew
he was sweet on me. The way
some people will behave.
She could be the very devil,
so I disliked her very much.
That's all I need
to say about that.

Emma Goes Back to the Home-place

We canned two bushels of peaches.
There are lots of tomatoes
for eating but they're not
ripening too fast so we can
keep up with them. We don't
have the flowers we used to.
My husband Will's garden was full
of dill and he's been fighting it
all summer. I made dill pickles,
though I can't eat them. I want
to finish so I can replant violets.
I have two and three in a pot.

Last week I took a notion to get
some of mother's lamb's tail,
and figured it was still growing
down on the old home-place,
even though the land has been
fifty years wild, most of it
strip-mined. So yesterday we took
a ride down to Sherret. Things
have grown up something awful,
lots of farms have gone back.

We parked and I took Will back
the old lane, and at the bottom
of the mountain steps we found
a stand of those long white
blossoms—must have been a good
year for them, they were all over.
Mother had them up by the porch,
on the mountaintop, but now
they've seeded themselves below.

I dug down and got a good clump
and put it in a cardboard box.
We didn't go up to the old place.
The steps are gone, and I'm sure
the house is too.

Next we visited one of my old
girlfriends. She was married
to a friend of my first husband.
I haven't seen them since my son
was born nearly sixty years ago.
Even their neighbor knew me,
but for a while I kept them guessing.

I had been Sunday school secretary
and she was treasurer. When I told
her that, she had forgot. She has
turned kind of shaky. I said:
I am Emma Dobson, but I used to be
Peggy Lindsay, and before that
Margaret Woster. I didn't go
into how I got all those names,
but I was born Emma Margaret,
then each of my husbands called
me a name to go with theirs.

She knew me by my first and cried
My God and hugged me. I imagine
there's lots of folks I still know
all over down there, if I could
keep up with where they've gone.
I made them acquainted with Will.

From Emma's Scrapbook: 1929

She keeps this for her baby,
due in six months:

Take one and a half teaspoon lard
one and a half teaspoon pine tar
one and a half teaspoon dry mustard,
one and a half teaspoon sulfur,
one and a half teaspoon nutmeg.
Mix well in a dish. This is for
when the flu sits on the lungs.
Spread the mixture between doubled
muslin and apply as poultice on chest.
If properly applied, it will not burn
and is a splendid remedy and may
save many a life. We tried it
in 1918 with very good results.
A READER, January 19, 1929.

If only they had tried this
on her baby brother, she thinks,
though he died long after
the flu epidemic of 1918.

She has carried her own growing
cough for weeks, and as she cuts
out the remedy she feels her lungs
filling--her husband Dale gives her
chicory tea with honey,
one of old Annie Bender's
standbys, and it helps a bit.

She has nutmeg and mustard
in the pantry. She could trade

her fresh cinnamon rolls
to the railroad or canal men
for sulfur and pine tar.
Then the next day she brings
up all the congestion
in a great heave. No need
to waste spice or cloth.
Yet she can imagine her baby
coughing, only a season away,
so she keeps the remedy.
The concoction might need
to prove its promise in time.

Emma Makes It through the Depression

I've had many days like this,
when I didn't care if I got up,
but couldn't just stay in bed.
My husband Will doesn't know.

In the thirties, when I was first
married to Dale, the men didn't
make much, though things were
cheaper. I made some by washing
clothes for the canal men.
Did shorts at ten cents,
long johns got me twelve,
and that was over a washboard.
I still use my washboard some,
a glass one—wore out I don't
know how many. Heated water
on a coal stove I used
for cooking and baking too.
Been using gas now for years.

Dale made sixteen dollars a week,
and I did too, for about two years,
though lots of days I thought
I'd never last. Now is a better
time—don't want those days back.

When Dale died I was surprised,
not sad right off, just startled,
but that is the way of it.
How could working hard be
the death of you? I'm here,

and Will is here still and
we've worked awful hard.
Right now Will is planting
lettuce and peas. I am
busy making an afghan.

From Emma's Scrapbook: 1938

Her son Andy's teacher,
Mr. C.A. Conley, sent home
a page of the boy's handwriting,
and a picture of a sailing ship
he colored. The ship is under
a blushed setting or rising sun,
the ocean is smeared with violets,
the saffron sails are as proud
and full as pregnant aprons.

But the script is what makes
her wonder what they are
teaching the boy, what odd
new words have been trying him.
Fourth grade, already a class
beyond what his father passed,
and his uppercase letters look
like fine buildings in town,
laced and painted in three colors.
His lowercase script shirks
across the page like ants
trailing some rumored sweetness.
The wispy line of numerals
were an afterthought.

*This is a sample of my best
handwriting*, it says below,
and she is sure it is, sure
it will never be as fine
as this again. She folds
the ruled paper eight times,
and puts it away in her book.

Emma Waits out a Spring Snow

We sure had some snow.
So many wrecks, all over
the road, down ditches
and spun out in fields
like cars which had gotten
loose without their drivers.

Didn't go out ourselves,
only for the mail or to feed
the horses, and Will does that.
All I do is crochet and cook.
Will goes out to feed the cats,
two nice black females. One
meets him right at the door.

Before the snow Will had onions
and lettuce up, and some peas.
Also have tomato plants but
we kept them indoors. Now
the Easter flowers are coming
through. I wonder why I quit
going to church. Been all
of forty years now. Everything

might be froze—it's all snowed
over. My mother would say that
early planting was like trying
to get ahead of God.

Emma Hopes for Her Great-Grandson

I am trying to get my spring cleaning
done. The kitchen's in good shape.
Will and I did cupboards. I washed
the dishes. I have a lady to do

walls, woodwork, and the cellar.
The Easter flowers are coming on,
pushing up like fingers. Last week
my son Andy, his wife, Luella,

my granddaughter and her baby
Eddie visited. He's quite
the little man. Had a big time
getting into my Easter basket.

I don't keep candy in it,
just crocheted chicks and rabbits,
but he opened all the plastic eggs
and threw straw in the air.

He sure eats good, which all kids
don't. I remember when the boys
came home from the War, such good
men, hit the beach on D-Day, fought

their way through God-knows-what
clear to Berlin. When they got home,
decorated, tough, lean, there was no
helping the young girls. They were

smitten. I hope Eddie never has to
go fight Nazis or whoever comes next.
You never know what will pop up.

All he knows are shapes and colors,

but that's all he needs to follow
a flag. We did what we had to
back then, and I hope it was enough.
That little boy is walking already.

From Emma's Scrapbook: 1944

Too many died in the world war
for Emma to save the obituaries,
instead she keeps the clipping
about the deserter gunned down
on Liberty Street, right beside
her and Dale's house in Clarion.
Dale says, *Enough is enough,*

swears that when he retires
they will move to the forty acres
on Scotch Hill. Any excuse to leave
town, Emma thinks. She's of two
minds about moving back to a farm
—half of her likes being away
from the work she's always known.

The Clarion News says the man
claimed to be *a veteran
of the Pacific campaign,
incapacitated by malaria,*
that he traveled all over,
always keeping a full tank,
a shotgun in his trunk,
and *a revolver on his person.*

Where the man made his mistake
was in trying to settle down.
A man like him has to run,
Emma thinks, has to keep
his steps soft, his picture
out of sight, not take a job
driving dozer at the mines.
He should have gone out West

like her brother, and never
got found. Emma was startled
by the gunshots next door,
the police lights pinwheeling
and chasing the air ahead.
She wishes he had vanished,
had not reminded her that those
who are running might be right
beside you, might be somewhere
you are trying hard to live.

From Emma's Scrapbook: 1947

Some of those poor boys
they sent to Germany have
left part of their bodies
over there, Emma thinks,
but still they get them
up and walking on fake
feet, knees and legs.
Today in the *Post Gazette*,
Dick Reddinger is walking
right on the front page.
His leg and hand are plastic,
and the world is now full
of plastic, and the injured.

The paper does not explain
the look on Reddinger's face
as he walks past his buddies,
men using two canes, men
without noses or lips,
which the camera avoids,
like Bob Lindsay's son
Delbert, who finally died
despite his father's prayers,
and him a preacher.

And thank God for that,
Emma thinks, thank God
they needn't use plastic
for all of that.

Emma believes a man should
go out swinging an axe,
like her first husband.

He could never have lived
with half a body,
would not even pay attention
to his heart sending its dull
telegrams down his arms: *A body
is never as sound as it looks.*

Emma Complains about Will

He was eighty on Saturday,
and sometimes he treats me
like I'm the one older,
even though I'm a whole
year behind him. Well,
maybe I'm not doing good
at times—my knees bother
me so that I don't garden
as much because I can't
walk on uneven ground,

but I know enough to know
you can't catch fish
in a pond where a man throws
in food everyday like he does,
like he was feeding chickens
in the yard. The water
just boils next to him
when he walks the banks.
There's some big ones
in there, and Will wants them
for the table, but he's gone
and tamed them. They ain't
hungry and won't take bait,
but he doesn't listen. I try
to tell him, but I might
as well save my breath.

Today I'm doing the taxes.
Will won't ever do the bills,
says he's never filled out
a single check in his life.
What'd he do fifteen years ago,

before he met me? Send cash?
I wouldn't be surprised.

After my first husband died,
I waited until it was decent,
then started going down
to the square dances.
That's where I met Will
—oh he was in the eye of all
the girls. Tall, straight,
had his own teeth, hair dark
mostly. He was considered
quite the catch, but I got him.
Now he's the one who's going
to catch it if he doesn't
straighten up. A real horse's
leg, which is worse because
that's where it all runs down.

I can get up in the morning,
get four loaves of bread out
of the oven and have the pans
all washed by seven.
Not many women can do that.
Will's up by then too, feeds
the horses, then watches me
over coffee. It's just as well
he's not much on talking
first thing in the morning.
And he knows enough to know
when to leave me be.
If he ever had something
to say about my baking
he'd only say it once.

Even though it's spring
we had snow again today.
Will has cabbage, lettuce
sweet onions and peas
in the ground. I told him
it was too early for making
garden, and his fertilizer was
was too hot, but he won't listen,

like when he burned brush
down by the ponds, in March.
He acted like he didn't hear
me then either. He had
a big pile of sumac,
cow's tongue, elderberry,
and a bunch of prickers.
All morning he was at it,
with a scythe and pitchfork.

It went up like a house afire.
I looked down there and about
slipped my gear, I was so upset,
flames shooting up twenty feet.

It's March, I said, *Ever hear
of wind in March?* Sometimes
I just want to take his head off.
He said something about having
to get work done when he was able,
or something like that, I didn't
catch it. But he could have
burned down the barn. He didn't,
but he could have, easy as not.

From Emma's Scrapbook: 1921

The article is titled
That Missing Salesman
and it tells about
the women's goods salesman
who disappeared years ago.
She plans to write the writer
Marben Graham, and tell
what she and nearly half
of Washington County knows.

In Pittsburgh, Graham says,
someone claims he had run
up gambling debts in Wheeling,
but the owner of Herman's
a juke joint on the Ohio,
says he repaid it all
but 15 dollars, not enough
he says, to track him down
through the frosted hemlocks
and hollows in the boondocks.

The man is dead all the same.
His body can be found somewhere
up on Lost Stocking Ridge.
They've seen his wares spread
from the treetops, like nests
of crows which have escaped
from the circus. But how could
they know that down in the city?

Emma knows and Herman knows
he won't ever see his money.
The bootleggers got him

and what was lining his pockets.
That man just rode the wrong way
up the wrong ridge, Emma thinks.
It could happen to anyone
in these hills full of wrong
turns, full of the missing.

Emma Goes to a Reunion

I feel pretty good for 79 years.
Will and I went to the Lindsay
reunion last week—my first husband
Dale's family. My son Andy and his
family went too, and Minnie,
Dale's little sister, arranged it
at the state park, under one
of those covered picnic spots.
In my day we'd have met on
the family farm, but the old
Lindsay place is long gone,
like our home-place. That's
a funny notion: *My day*.
It's as though these days belong
to someone else, and I'm just
allowed in like a visitor.

Everyone brought a dish.
I took my chicken and noodles
and dumplings—one of last year's
pullets. We finally have a good
coop full. Last year's chickens
weren't much good for laying
and I had to go to the Amish
for eggs. They weren't as nice.

Dale's Scotch kin liked my food
well enough—I brought back
an empty pan. Even his older
sister Alice ate some—usually
she won't eat anyone else's cooking.
She's an odd one. She was married
for a month fifty years ago,

left with a man for Pittsburgh,
then came back and said she was
never married, even kept her name.
She stayed single after that.
A lot of Dale's people were
like that, a bit funny in the head.

Well, everyone had a nice time.
At the end of the day, Minnie
gave out prizes. One went to
them living the farthest away,
one to the youngest, another
to the oldest. They started
to give that one to Alice, but
like Will says, I piped up.
Should have kept my mouth shut,

I said, *There's one older!*
and they couldn't deny it,
though it was my new husband
and I only used to be an in-law
when I was married to Dale.
Most didn't even know Will's name.
Minnie gave him the knick-knack shelf
anyway, and he gave it to Alice.

I hope they aren't all mad at me.
It is awfully nice of them
to invite us. But Will was older
than any, I don't care who says what.
He had no business giving that shelf
back to Alice even if to most
of them he was a stranger.

From Emma's Scrapbook: 1950

Nabbed the photograph caption says,
a smashed police car and a dead
deer lolling across the hood.

Police chief Volpe gave her
son Andy such a hard time when
he was young, once arresting him

when he and Brad Johnson cut down
parking meters with a hacksaw
and put them in Volpe's cruiser

because he had given them parking
tickets—they were only high
spirited and Volpe couldn't prove

a thing. Chief Volpe wasn't hurt
in the accident, but his cruiser was
destroyed when the button buck leapt

through the windshield. He had
to get Lucius Lowry to tow him
into town, and everyone looked

at him, sitting in Lucius' truck,
his precious Plymouth looking
like someone punched it in the face.

It was 1950 and Emma's Andy
was serving in Korea, while Volpe
had avoided fighting in the last

war by declaring he was an only

son. Andy was Emma's only child,
yet Chief Volpe got out of the fray.

As far as Emma is concerned, Joe Volpe
is a cowardly bastard, and the deer
was a slap in the face, a reproach

to those like him who claimed to serve
the law then stretched it to suit
themselves. She doesn't forgive easily,
if at all, and the day she went down
to the jail to get Andy she all but
took Volpe's head off right there.

Ever since, Emma swore if she saw him
crossing the street and she was driving,
she'd have him draped across her hood.

From Emma's Scrapbook: 1953

She had heard it happen,
heard the bone break
as it happened and did not
need to read the account.
Still she kept the clipping,
though God only knows why.
The strap snapped, the one
holding her son to the top
of the power pole.

Andy became a lineman,
climbing and wiring
after a hot summer
of scaling trees, trimming
the tops to let in light
so they could make a movie
starring Gary Cooper.
Andy was agile and fearless
like his father, and proud
of his job, of making more
than the boys who stayed
in town and worked,
safe at Western Auto
or Brown's Boots and Shoes.

It snapped and he fell,
and she heard his fingers
scrape the cross arm
as he tried to hold onto
the 30 foot pole, heard him
curse all the way to the ground
hitting Bob McClain on the head
with his flailing arms, heard

him hit the ground and land on
his feet, bounce once and fall

again and break his wrist.
For years he woke in the night
with a shout, reliving
the moment he knew he was
going down, and she heard
that too, heard it
each and every time.

Emma Is Surprised while Doing Chores

I have to get my picture
taken for my license tomorrow,
so I'm getting my hair cut
today—it sure did grow over
the winter, the only thing
that does. It's going to be
a busy few days. When
I get back from town there
will be wash to do
and that will make me
plenty tired. I still like
to use my old ringer washer
because I know the clothes
are done up right when
I put them through the wringer.
That new washer my son bought me
is all water and spinning and when
it shuts off and I open the door,
I find all the clothes twisted.
That can't be good for them.

The Amish man is coming soon
to trim the horses' hooves,
so I'll have to watch out
for him while I work.
He spooks me when he comes up
from behind when I'm weeding
or something. They drive no
cars and make no noise
when they arrive. You just get
going on something and then

there's a voice and a man
with a beard and black clothes.
It's enough to make you jump
clear out of your skin.

There was suddenly lots to do
yesterday when we had company.
My son and his wife and
my husband Will's brother
Walt and his wife dropped in.
They stayed for two meals.
I had oyster stew and hickory
baked ham and cheese sandwiches,
with sweet onion and lettuce,
at noon. It wouldn't occur
to them how much work it takes
to lay out that much food.
I had pork spare ribs, kraut,
dumplings, creamed new peas
and potatoes for supper.

So I didn't do much today.
I rested and played Old Sol
some (even beat him, twice,
and I never cheat), after
I baked bread. Always do
that in the morning before
the day heats up. I will
have to get some yarn
and get busy on something
after I finish the rag rug
for in front of my sink.
Could as easy buy one,
but they're made so cheap
you might as well spread

the newspaper on the floor,
and they never last. I use
good denims, heavy cotton cut
out of Will's work shirts,
and then I put in colors
from my old house dresses,
enough to make the eye dance.
My rugs will wear and wear,
no matter how hard you use
them, and in front of my sink
a rug can go back to rags
right under my feet
before I know it.

From Emma's Scrapbook: 1967

She remembers the old hotel
in Kittanning, the one
pictured in the historical
clipping, recalls the day
of the temperance mob raid.

On that warm evening
of June 1918, the Kittanning
fire bell rang, drawing
several men up Market Street,
pulling the two wheeled
hose cart, with the bell
clanging with every
revolution of the wheels.

Unidentified gunmen
were firing shots from
the second story windows
as a crowd pushed forward.
Someone had thrown a torch.

Her father was in that tavern,
having sold some horses,
and now Emma and her mother
waited outside—he had only
gone in for a minute, he said,
for a taste to clear his throat.

The men with the hose company
sprayed it, but too late.
The police arrested some young
soldiers—too young to drink
her mother said, but they were

going to France, though
she didn't then know what
that meant. Emma was too young
to remember much more, or to know
why they burned the hotel down.

Emma Butchers

Today my husband Will and I
did up fifty chickens.
Not many can do that,
from pecking to freezing
all in one day. Will did
the heads and I scalded,
gutted and put them up.

They were nice-sized birds
for baking or with noodles.
Will never butchered chickens
this early, but I talked
him into it. They're better
younger. He used to let them
get older, then he'd brag:

Some were 25 pounds,
but they'd be as tough
as your boot and fit
only for soup. Now
I get tender pullets.
Will's problem is he can't
stand not letting something
grow as big as it can get.
Some farmers are that way.

We used to butcher chickens
back on my old home-place,
then pack the meat in jars,
or in crocks sealed over
with their own fat
—we'd half cook them first.
We kept the crocks in a cave

where it was always cool.

My brother Jack would cut off
the heads, and I think
he liked the business a little
more than what was right.
He'd grab the squawking birds,
whack off their heads, then
throw the bodies in the yard.
Before long there'd be
a crowd of chicken carcasses
all around him, running
and falling on the ground
like children playing tag.
Jack would laugh whenever
he let another one loose.
Even then I scalded them,
mother and I—you couldn't
get my sister Olivia near
a chicken. Too good for it.

But Will does his chickens
different—my, that man has
a soft touch for killing.
He grabs them by the leg
with a long wire, then pulls
them out of the coop.
They carry on something
fierce at first. A chicken
only has two gears:
content or afraid.

Then he pulls them under
his arm and strokes them
until they start to cluck.

He won't kill a chicken
until it calms down,
otherwise the meat is strong
he says, and I believe him.
Next he ties their legs,
slips their heads between
two nails sticking out
of a stump, then lets loose
with his hatchet. But he
doesn't let them flop,
which he says bruises
the meat—he hangs them

by their feet from the branches
of the peach tree where
they flap and drain and
get it over with. Sometimes
the tree will be full of them,
a flock perched upside down,
like a bunch of big white bats.
It's quite a sight.

Boiling water takes out most
of the feathers, scraping
with a knife gets the rest.
I bag the liver, neck and heart
and stuff them back inside
—then in the deep freeze
they go. They're not dead
fifteen minutes before
I have them all done up.

From Emma's Scrapbook: 1949

In August 1949, they found
Emma's brother's sedan,
at least she thinks it is:

Old Man Clarion River has
been revealing some secrets
during the past week after
the lowering of the depth
by 22 feet for the repair
of the hydro-electric dam
six miles downstream.

She half-expected them to find
Jack inside, but they said
the broken window makes some
believe that someone may have
escaped the machine when
it plunged into the forty foot
deep channel. Nothing was said

about the bullet holes
she had seen when he drove
up her lane, saying he had
to go away, was as good
as dead. They also found
a case of bootleg in the trunk,
and men dived off the banks
in search of more.

Jack was too smart, Emma knew,
to leave the plates on the car,
and he was far too slick to have
gone down with it—he probably

propped the accelerator pedal
with a stick and watched
as the car ran down the hill
and over the bank on a curve.
Jack would have thought it
through, and the bootleg would
be his signature for those
he wanted to believe him dead.

But Emma didn't believe it,
not for a minute, some secrets
even the river does not know.

Emma Buries the Dead

To start I might as well say it.
Buck died, the younger horse.
Will went down to the barn
to feed them and there he was,
on his side in the straw.

So I called Will's grandson Jeff.
He brought the high lift and dug
a grave for him. They put him
in with the machine, then
jumped in to straighten him out.
They left his halter. You must
leave the halter on your horse
so those ahead know he meant
something. We both feel

pretty bad about it. He hadn't
been good at times and this time
he didn't make it back around.
I just don't want to talk about it.

We have the new pond dug out,
all but a little. A fellow
is coming back to finish it
—then the spring will keep
the new and old pond fresh.

Old Pal sure misses Buck.
He stands in his stall,
rubs the wall. Yesterday
before the storm, he walked
circles around the pond.

From Emma's Scrapbook: 1956

May 15, 1956.
Dear Mrs. Lindsay,
Your Bill for Work on Lots
in the Cemetery includes:
Dirt and Hauling: $2.
Seeds and Fertilizer: $1.
Labor on your Dad and Mother: $8.
Labor on Child: $4.
Sincerely, Leroy Haufman
Sherret, RD #1, Penna.

Emma pays it right away,
and then wonders where
the money will come from
down the road, when no one
remembers her home-place,
who will keep the graves
full of geraniums, cutting
them back and saving them
over the winter to be used
again, who will replace
Leroy, who is himself getting
up in years. She is determined

this will never happen,
that perennial care must be
assumed by her son Andy.
She will simply tell him,
that she wants petunias on
her baby brother's grave,
a little stone is all
he has, saying *Baby Freddie.*

And she wants to check up
on Leroy, see if he has kept
the grass away from the base
of her parents' stone,
where she ordered carved:

Death is a tribute due,
that I have paid,
and so must you.

From Emma's Scrapbook: 1972

They used Will's silver saddle
and his horse in a picture
for the Farmer's Mutual calendar.
They took it in the pasture,
the young woman posed alongside.
She was afraid of the animal
though he was always gentle,
and wouldn't move as long
as Will stood off camera
holding out a marshmallow.

She's dressed in a red western
fringed shirt, blond hair tucked
under a red hat, and behind them,
in the picture from the calendar,
is sagebrush and ponderosa pine,
not Pennsylvania sumac and maple,
not a pond full of bass.
They added everything later,
Emma knows, but wonders how.

She has on leather gloves,
and holds Pal's reins. Will
stood there across the fence
and she held her smile.
She has a big shiny buckle,
and Emma could tell she never
held a horse before
The silver saddle glows
like it was in a movie.

Emma Laments before Taking Her Medication

We had some ups and downs
with my niece Judy's son
getting killed. A car.
Judy has always been good
to me. She'll stop by,
take my blood pressure,
check my medicine, run me
out to the doctor. She makes
sure I don't overlook anything.

Will got the flu and then
I got it from him. I wasn't
as bad as he was. Yesterday
I talked to my son Andy
and—he's not feeling so good.
It's rough having aches and pains
I sure have had my share.

I didn't do much canning
or jelly-making this year.
There were no pears,
no greengages.
Very few apples.

The fish sure are growing.
Will and I went to the game
commission and got 500 bass
for the ponds. Hope they
make it. The bullfrogs
Will stocked last year
got huge, with meaty legs,

then they all hopped away.
He was so mad I still
can't say *frog* around him.

I got up at four this morning.
Wrote and went back to bed
after two hours. I got up
again in the light, took two
pain-killers and a nerve pill
and felt pretty good all day.

Emma Regrets the Way Her Mother Died

My mother passed away
on the 21st of this month,
1932. My son Andy wasn't quite
three years old and full
of the old Nick. The night
she died he was playing
around the coal stove
in the sitting room
of the old home-place.
He didn't understand
what was happening,
that mother was lying
upstairs leaving us all.
Father was sitting there,
and Andy was his favorite,
no one could correct him
when father was around.

Once when I was a girl,
we were riding home in a wagon,
and came up on a man whipping
a black horse by the side
of the road. It was wild
with fear, and slick with lather.

There's no call for that,
my father said, but the man
said he should mind his own
business unless he wanted
some of the whip himself,
which is what he shouldn't

have said. Father jumped
down from the wagon, took
the whip from him and
gave him a piece of it.
Then he took the near-crazed
horse home with us and no
one ever said a word to him
about it, not even the law.

Well, he was the same way
about my son. Everyone
was upset, with mother dying
and all, but Andy started
cutting up something awful
—he knew father would protect
him. My sister Olivia
yelled at him and he called
her an old witch, which was true.

Then he said he had to use
the outhouse, that one of us
had to take him out back.
We told him to wait.
He danced around and then
threatened to do it against
the stove. We were so caught up
in mother's death I don't think
we even heard him. So Andy made
up his mind to relieve himself,
and burnt himself against
the iron stove—Oh did he
let out a howl. My father
started laughing, then Olivia,
and finally we were all gone
to tears. Mother was in

the middle of dying while
we laughed downstairs.
It has bothered me ever since.

From Emma's Scrapbook: 1930

George Collier signed her mother
and father's marriage certificate
in 1890, in Sherret. Her mother
was then young Maggie Myers,
four children in her future.

Collier was a Methodist minister
and buried Maggie 42 years later.
Emma saves the paper, pulled out
of the family Bible before the book
was lost when her sister Olivia
sold everything, their parents gone.

After Emma leaves the home-place,
her mother begins writing her:

Dear Em and famley,
Hope youns are all well.
Livy has a sore thum so
I thought I would rite and
tell you if you are coming
out on easter your brother
Jack and Flossie are coming
Sunday afternoon. You could
come out with them as Father's
car is on the bum, or he mite
get it fixed up afore then.

Thairs quite a bit of sickness
aroun so hope to hear from you
or see you soon. Hope the boy
and Dale are all well. Mother.

But they never make Easter dinner
as her husband Dale had to clear ice
from the Mahoning railroad bridge
after a bad spring storm.
Olivia's thumb healed quickly.

Dear Em and famley,
We are all as usel. Hoping
youns are all well. This is
a fine day, suppose you will
 think of making garden. Livy
is ironing and Father is busy
with the horses, he still has
a passel. He got his car
going in good shape and Jack
got another one in good shape,
a big one. He has no work yet,
if you want to come out father
can bring you as Jack might
have no way of getting gas,
though he always seems to get
aroun. Closing for now.
Suppose your boy is busy.
Hope to hear from you soon.
Mother.

Not long after Jack runs away
from Flossie, and her mother's
health slips then flees, and Emma
comes to stay, with her son,
for the last two weeks.
Her father spoils the boy.

She does not remember ever
writing back, but she does

remember pall bearers
carrying her mother down
the mountain steps, and her
worrying that the body
would slide to the bottom
of the box, that she'd be
buried with her knees bent,
as though giving birth.

Then she puts that out of her head,
recalling instead them all singing
*Safe in the Arms of Jesus, Going
Down in the Valley,* and *Face to Face.*
Even her son crowed away, off key,
but he sang, his good suit crimped
in the heavy starch she used.

From Emma's Scrapbook: 1946

She presses a flower
in a remembrance card
from her father's funeral
in 1946. She puts it
between the obituaries
from the papers in Kittanning
and Clarion. He was living
in her house, where he never
wanted to die, Emma knew,
years after her mother died,
when he got what they called
the wandering mind and had
to leave the farm, Her sister
Olivia wanted him sent away,
so Emma took him herself.

For a while he trained horses
for a neighbor in Sherret,
always a man to love animals.
After he slipped too much
even for this job, he'd ask
about the mares and her son
Andy would pretend to go
to the stables to see them.

They're fine, gramps, he'd say,
coming back from an idle hour
spent in town, and her father
would thank him and be content.

He sat on their porch and smoked
his pipe or at the Loomis Hotel
drinking whiskey, *something to cut*

the phlegm. He'd argue
about the war in Europe,
how they had to stay out
of the trenches like the first.
He'd start awful squabbles,

and Emma would send her son
to get him before the old man
thrashed someone with his cane.
Then he started falling asleep
on the glider with a lit pipe,
so Emma went to the A&P to ask
them not to sell him matches.
He never caught on as the clerks
said they were being rationed.

When the war was over he died,
and the family gathered,
even her sister Olivia,
whom Emma knew would not lift
a finger to help her father.
There were more nephews
and nieces than she could
keep up with. They all sang
The Sweet By-and-By and
*When the Roll Call Is Called
up Yonder*, and two preachers
said words. That was in all

the papers, but not how
the horses shied behind fences
along the route the hearse took,
their hides full of quivers,
how the flowers smelled
of kerosene and coal,

how the church ceiling
did not fall when Olivia
paid her feeble respects.

Emma Fights Getting Older

The Amish get away with having
outside toilets like we used
when I was a girl, but we can't
—not that I would want one.
I guess our township supervisor
is going to stir up some trouble
about it—something about water.
At least that's what my husband
Will heard in town yesterday.
I'll read about it in the paper.

The Dutchmen have been coming
from out by Harrisburg, buying
up farms here after the old folks
leave the traces and their sons
want no part of farming. Guess
I can't blame them—it's plain
hard work and you never have
two dimes to rub together.
No wonder Will's son drives
those big lumber trucks instead
of working the farm Will gave him.
They rent out the fields,
or they'd all be head high.

The corn is still in the fields,
drooping. No one could get it in
before frost with all that rain.
This weather is more than I can
take, the cold came too early.
I had to go to the doctor
for a shot in my arm. The cold
made it so I couldn't use it.

Will is riding my stand-still bike.
I ride it a lot. I never said much
to anyone about it, but for a while
I could hardly walk. Now I am back
with my old doctor and feeling good.
Will just came out of the pantry.
He says he rode the bike for a mile.

Could be worse. My sister-in-law
Flossie lived in Kittanning but now
has to stay in a nursing home.
She'll be 86 the 27th of this month.
Jack, her husband and my brother,
was two years older, nine years more
than me. The other doctor told me
I needed to have my eye operated on,
and I was so upset I about slipped
my gear. I had them both tested
at the clinic—they said I had
20-20 with my glasses on,
but the right is a little bad,
it watered a lot and bothered me.

Now I can see real good and am
glad for it. That other doctor
was dead wrong. I can ride standing
still more than a mile anytime
I want, work all day. I'm as strong
as I've ever been. I could work
circles around those Amish women,
though they do it all the hard way.

From Emma's Scrapbook: 1980

The *Oil City Derrick* publishes
a seasonal picture on page one,
two tilted corn cribs stuck
in a snow drifted field
among the Amish in Lancaster,
cousins to those who live

around her. The stark photograph
reminds her of their old ways.
It breaks her husband Will's heart
to see the Amish buying up all
the farms on each side of them,
good farms—but that's not
the problem, as they are good
farmers. But those homesteads
were cleared and built-up
during Will's lifetime,
adding indoor plumbing, electric
and telephones and now the Amish
tear it all out, decades
of hard work gone in a week.

Then they hang their dark
blue clothes on the line,
lace on the windows and get
on with their plain lives.

For Emma, for Will,
this is another *going back*,
the same as when a field
is abandoned to brush.
Once something is done right,
it should stay done.

That undoing of light and water
is a pure and simple waste,
nothing plain about it except
for plain foolishness, at least
as far as Emma can tell.

Emma Sneaks in Some Writing

I must mark on a calendar
when I last write, as I forget
what I have to say or said.

We had turkey and noodles
for Thanksgiving. In August
I got a forty pounder—used
to be you could only get them
over the holidays, now they sell
them anytime at all. It was
a big bird. I roasted it
overnight and when it was cool
took all the meat off the bone
and put it up in snap plastic
containers in the deep freeze.
It made a lot, and tasted good.

We never raised turkeys back
on our old home-place, we shot
wild ones. A dumber animal
never drew breath. Whole flocks
would come right up to the house,
and come back again and again
like they were aiming to deliver
themselves. When they say
that someone *doesn't have
the sense God gave a goose,*
they ought to be saying *turkey.*

My husband Will is taking
a nap after supper, so I am
sitting quiet and writing
Christmas cards. The TV girl

said only eleven days. My hand
cramps when I have to sit still
and write inside cards. I tell
them all the same news over again.

From Emma's Scrapbook: 1927

Myrtle Young has died,
and Emma keeps the clippings.
They lie in her lap now,
three long columns,
stretched out like tongues.

They say she jumped
from Clarence Stoy's car
at thirty miles an hour.
Emma knew Myrtle when they sat
in the fourth grade row,
Myrtle better at sums,
Emma at history. When she died
she was only twenty and Emma
was a year into her marriage.
Myrtle was engaged to Stoy,
whose whole family lived on
three farms at Stoy's Crossing,
not a mile from where she leapt,
allegedly the paper says.

Stoy now sits in the Kittanning jail,
where Emma imagines him singing out
his grief or his story: They had
quarreled, Myrtle did not want
to go home so early. *The couple
had been keeping company for over
a year, and were greatly attached.*

Myrtle was not reckless, Emma knows.
She must have been tallying
something, and the coroner says
it was months, not miles per hour.

Stoy says he was not paying
attention to what she was saying,
turning to her only when he heard
I'll get even with you, and when
he felt the air rushing in,
and heard her body
landing on the dirt road.

There are so many Stoys now
at Stoy's Crossing, all red-headed.
At harvest they trail across
the fields, looking like clumps
of Seneca paintbrush, and Emma
doesn't suppose they'll grieve
much the loss of one more.

Emma Has Her Say

Will was listening to TV
and I've been trying to get
some writing done. He is
sound asleep now and won't
be able to sleep tonight.
I never can, so we'll
just keep each other company.
I tell him stories at night
and he never complains.
He is good to talk to,
and sometimes I talk and talk,
and sometimes he does too.
It's got so I can tell
from his breathing if he's
listening or sleeping.
When he draws deep and seldom
he's out--then I really start
in, and get to tell it all.

Emma on Her Eightieth Birthday

Today we are going down
to the home place with flowers
for the graves. I'm not
so old, just slowing up.
I remember well, too well.
My doctor says: *Rest is good*
medicine for high blood pressure.
I play out easy and wonder
if my glasses are close enough
to my face. I feel I have always
been this way. Can't get over

Will finding one horse dead
last spring. Odd the younger
went first, and to think on it.
Will's youngest brother Bernard
died when he fell in fishing.
His oldest brother Bum jumped in
after. Young Bernie's boots filled

and he went down to the water.
That was what killed Bum later,
younger than me, lying drunk
beside a heap of western novels
in a rented room he didn't
keep very clean either.
Bum never got the water out
of his throat, Will says.
Couldn't drink it down.

Have an old friend who's pretty
bad, but everyone likes her.
Her daughter wants them to take

her license away because she
turns corners and hits cars,
then says, *I only took a little
paint off.* I tell her
if she ever hits mine I will
have her in the jug.

That's what you say, she answers.
She's real bad, and not as old.
All I have for trouble are knees.

She likes her smokes and drinks,
drives her daughter almost bugs.
I'll bet she doesn't remember
everything like I do.

From Emma's Scrapbook: 1951

Her nephew Robert Lindsay
has taken up the pulpit,
and his toothy face appears
in *The Kittanning News Leader*
as he is one of those who
will speak on *The Challenges*
Christian Men Face Today.
Behind him is the brick wall
of the A&P he manages,
and he looks so like her
only son she wonders whether
he might be a purer version
of him, born so the world
might live and all sinners
find redemption. He looks
like he would not fall
to temptation, would be
delivered from evil. Robert
looks like his A&P is full
of our daily bread, and might
forgive hungry shoplifters
Robert Lindsay looks a member
of a wedding, the perennial
best man, like he might burst
into flame or even make all
Kittanning holy in an afternoon.

Emma Hangs on to What She Can

When father died, my sister
Olivia made us sell
the home-place and I was glad
mother was not buried there,
but up nearer town. We sold
the land but kept the gas wells,
all other mineral rights went
to the coal company and they

stripped the whole 70 acres,
took out the trees, turned
the earth upside down. Ruined.

Then this week I get a note
saying I owe taxes on the wells
—just finished a letter
to the revenuer. The taxman
in Washington will sure be
surprised when he gets it.
Each well brings a dime a day.
I've never paid on them and
don't believe I'll start now.

When I'm making rugs I think
about mother. She taught me
how to stand up to things.
We sure had it hard,
and it was tougher after
I left—Olivia was all
for herself and not much help.
When I'm making rugs I remember

how tight mother made her knots,

showing me how to pull the rags
over the arms of a chair.
This week I've been having
trouble with my arms. I stop,

put on Ben-gay, and that helps,
unless the pain is too deep.
It's hard tying rags so I think
I will make myself a hat. I only
need my fingers to crochet.

Emma Lists a Few Certainties

If you want strong hands,
try wringing out your laundry
until you can't get another drop.

It's too long between times when
I see my family. My great-grandson
is growing up and out-of-sight.

I want to get another woman to help
me clean, but I'll have to find one
who can do it and take my bossing.

When I try to write on my lap,
my hand turns to chicken scratch.

Planting too early is all for naught.
My husband Will should learn that.

If you want a cat to catch vermin
in the barn, it has to stay in the barn.
Our cat Smokey would just disappear
but Will closes the hole he goes out.

When you're real sick like mother,
and you pass on, you're still
better off in the long run.

Getting old is a slowing up,
while dying is a letting go. You can't
do the first without the second.

I don't like TV. I can't follow
the stories while I sew. I get lost

in one or the other, and I'd rather
get lost in making something.

If you speak your mind you'll never
have to let anything fester
and get to you. But you'll find,
after a while, there's no one
left who'll listen to you.

Emma Gets Nostalgic

Will was down at the ponds today.
The one we just had dug is still
froze over, but the ice is gone
on the old one nearer the spring.
Now that the weather is better
we are going over to Clarion
to see the new river bridge.
Last week we went out to see
the new one over Gravel Lick.
Will keeps up on all the new
bridges and roads and he loves
to drive which is good. I don't.

I know those old bridges
were rickety and bad,
but I liked them better.
Now you come down the mountain
and sail right across that new
cement span without knowing.
If you didn't look to the side,
and Will can't when he's driving,
you wouldn't even know you were
going over the water at all.
The old ones were built on stone
and hung somehow--they called
them *suspended*. Riding over
them was like going in and out
of something, one place
to another, like a big
rib cage, or so I thought
when I first saw one as a girl.
That was when I thought Kittanning

was big and places like Clarion
or Pittsburgh were even farther.

Emma Endures the Dirt Track

When we were snowed in,
Will's grandson Jeff was
old faithful. He worked
all day hauling logs,
then plowed snow at our place.
Will wanted his grandsons to ride
horses with him, but they liked
tinkering with machines instead.
At their place, the farm across
the road, the one Will gave
his son, they have a wagon shed
full of about every wrench.

So they ride hot-rod buggies.
They even built a race track
for those three-wheel thingamajigs
—and the dust comes over here.

They all live on that farm,
the grandsons in house trailers.
The oldest, Bruce, has a wife
who is a real piece of work.
Not much account--but you'll
not catch me opening my mouth.
I hold my peace, about lots
of things. I know my business.

Will might stop riding Pal
in the parades. He's all
but quit saddling him now
—I'm sure he misses it,
but there comes a time.
Someday even his grandsons

will have to quit their track
—not that it bothers me.
They don't make noise for long.
No drinking is allowed
and when it's over they all
leave as quiet as you please.

Will Feeds the Livestock

I have been meaning to get
this down, but I keep putting
it off. We lost old Pal.
It was quick. Will went
down to the barn to feed him
some hay and oats and there

he was, standing in his stall.
He wouldn't eat, and just stood
there and stared at the wall.
Will put his hand on his nose.
It was cold. He said he put
his arm around his neck
for a minute, then called
the vet. Doc Lahr said
there was nothing he could do.
He was barely breathing.

He was standing almost dead
like a lightning struck
tree, still on his feet
—what a tough old fellow
he was. Will said
Give him a shot. The vet did,
and it was all over real soon.

The rest of this winter
we have had snow and more snow.
Will lays out an ear of corn
for a rabbit. He has to feed
something. The way the snow
is all beaten down outside
the back door I think there's

more than one. If we turn on
the porch light when he comes
up to the house, and look out,
we can watch him eat.

Emma Gets Around

Will traded the silver saddle
he rode on Pal in parades
for a new car, and we have
been going places. No sense
staying at home—we've been
having so much rain. No one
around here can make hay.
Can't get outside to work and

our garden is going up in the air.
So we went to a barbecue at Will's
brother's in New York State.
He does a hundred chickens
at a time, cooks for reunions
and weddings—then he invites
us for free eats. We went
in our new Chrysler Imperial.
It has

       a dark red inside,
       and the car itself
       is gray. It has
       four doors, eight
       cylinders, cruise
       drive, cold air,
       good heat and
       a locking gas cap.

We just got up one morning
and Will said he knew a fellow
at the dealer garage who'd take
the saddle in trade. We looked
at five different cars and liked

this one best. It gets

>thirty miles a gallon.
>Yesterday when it was
>so hot before the rain
>we had the cold air
>coming in. It rides
>like you're not moving.
>The seats adjust up
>and back and sideways.

My son Andy says
it was a good buy.

We got it in May and now
it is June and we have gone
2500 miles, so it's easy
to see we haven't been home
much. We went up to Tionesta
for the Independence Day parade.
The guy who got Will's saddle
has a horse what is too small
for it. It doesn't look near
as nice as it did on our palomino.

When Will rode that big saddle,
dressed in black, carrying
the flag, he looked all-American.
He was over six foot tall
back when he stood straight.
I always loved tall men.

Will Brings Home the Venison

The roads have been icy.
On Tuesday, Will drove me
to the hairdresser, then stopped
at the Boots and Saddle Club
to jaw with the other old farmers.
He had a glass of beer, or two,
and I wonder if that had something
to do with it. I don't say
anything when he has a drink,
not that I like it much.
He hardly ever does, so I keep
my peace. Well, on the way back
a deer jumped a fence. It flew
onto the hood, then back down
to the road. Will went about
a hundred feet, then looked back.

He said to himself: *I didn't
ask you to jump into me.*
So he backed up and found it
in a ditch. He threw it
in the trunk and drove home.

Will called his grandson Jeff
who hasn't been driving truck
since he caught his arm
on a log chain and got blood clots
and was in the hospital awhile.
They dressed and cut it up.
We only kept a hindquarter.
Jeff was glad for the rest
as money is tight for him and his.

When Will picked me up I teased him,
Do you have lunch ready? He laughed
and said, *No, but I've been busy
getting supper.* Then he told me.
I asked him if it hurt the new car.
No, he said, *Only slobbered up
the windshield.* It was a doe.

From Emma's Scrapbook: 1925

Emma could have saved Arthur Henry
had he not showed up when her sister
Olivia was hanging laundry
and Emma was still in the house,
getting ready *to receive* him,
as her mother called sitting
on the front porch all evening.
Her father called it *spooning*
and Emma thought that was truer,
as they talked a blue streak,
and served up heaps of sugar.

Olivia led Arthur to the porch
instead, and got him spring water
—he was always winded after
coming up the mountain steps.
Slim and dark, Olivia's figure
showed well when she reached up
to pin sheets and overalls.

Now Emma can only save his obituary:
*So flees this mortal soul/to seek
its home on high/Where ceaseless
ages roll/Amid glory in the sky.*
That was what it said
it said on his stone.

Olivia never meant to keep him,
as she was truly fit for no man,
though she later married Ray Mackin,
in what was called *A Quiet Wedding*
in the papers. She attended only
to see it happen, hear if anyone

would refuse to hold his peace.
They used the double ring ceremony,
and Emma knows it was a good thing.
It would take both to hold Olivia.

But when Arthur visited that day
up on the mountain, Olivia talked
him into berrying down the hill.
Emma sat on the porch until dusk.
She never knew for sure what went on
down there in the bushes, but
when Arthur returned a week later,

it was Olivia he asked after.
Her father told him Olivia
was not keeping company. Emma
watched out the window as he put
his hand on the boy's shoulder
and led him back to the steps.
Olivia was upstairs singing,
and Emma was sure Arthur heard
her as he went down the mountain.

So the boy was dead at seventeen:
The newspaper report was livid:

As nearly as could be determined,
the tragedy occurred about 1:00
Tuesday morning at the Helm's garage
within a stone's throw of his home.
They found him in the garage
where he worked, and ripped open
his shirt. Blood was pouring
from a bullet wound near his heart.

Emma has all the clippings.
They tell of those he left behind,
his mother and the other Henrys
who never knew what Emma knows.
She was the only one from her family
to attend the funeral, and she wore
her best dress. And she was
something to see, she thought.
Emma was something to behold.

Will Can't Eat but Emma Keeps Stocking Up

I've been up working since
five o'clock. Will is doing
pretty good but has been
awful sick. Still coughs
hard. Got his teeth all
pulled—the stitches come
out today. Eating is tough
for him, so I made eggs into
noodles—Will cut them
—then I cooked vegetable soup.
Now I want to bake some pies,
but I'll have to freeze them
—got a bushel of apples
and can't let them spoil.

Managed to go out for groceries
and such when Will was sick.
I want to drive more and Will
just tells me *take the car
and go,* but I feel so lost
by myself in that big Chrysler,
the trunk swallows up all
the groceries. But I don't want
to get away from driving.
Easy enough to lose something
without outright giving up.
After Will gets his choppers,
he might be able to eat again.
The deep freeze is near bursting.

Emma Mails off Her Pickle Recipes: Letter on Back

I. *Fourteen Day Pickles*

Thought I'd get these in an envelope

> *Wash pickles & place in crock.*
> *To each gallon of pickles*
> *add one cup salt,*

And down to the box at the road
So you get started while they're in season.
The one on top I used to make with mother
In late August on the farm
In Kittanning, when I was little.

> *cover with cold water.*
> *Let set one week, stir*
> *daily from bottom up,*

Those days would start out
Cool, crisp, but before long

> *wash out salt*
> *& split them*

The black of frost
Would show larger each morning.

> *but not clear to the end.*

I loved those days because
For at least half of them

Be sure to split
pickles. Pour boiling water

Until I was eleven, I would be
Off to school, see folks
I hadn't seen since spring planting,

> *over them, enough to*
> *cover, replace crock lid,*
> *let set one day.*

as they lived a few hollows over.
At about sixteen it used to mean
I'd get to see Dale regular.

> *Next day drain & to each gallon of pickles,*
> *sprinkle one tablespoon*
> *of powdered alum over top*

Then he finished all the schooling
He wanted. All winter he had
Talked big about a job off the farm,
In town or with the railroad.
I believed him as my heart
Had to, and as I guess

> *& cover with boiling water,*
> *let stand one day again.*

He had to believe himself.
And it wasn't all pipedream,
Just the beauty of a future away.

> *Next day, drain each gallon*

And then there was a beauty
In that man himself. He could be
Both sweet and wild,

      & make a syrup
      of four cups sugar

And when I learned how
To come to him, and he to me,
I found all the force

      & two quarts vinegar
      (full strength). Let this

I believed a part of union
Was softened by the moment.

      come to a boil & pour over.

He'd been squirreling away
Money in a canning jar,

      This is enough for
      one gallon.

Hidden in a hollow stump.
His father would claim it all
If he didn't. He waited, working

      Let stand one day

Nights, threshing wheat, mending tackle,
While I kept busy putting up the extra

& pour off into pan,
add one cup of sugar
for each gallon & heat.

From the garden, fighting
With my sister Olivia, lazy
Even now. She'd just as soon tell you

Do this for three days.

What to do as do it herself.

On the last day,

Finally Dale said he had enough,

put pickles into jars,

Pulled 100 dollars from the jar,

heat syrup to boil,

Told his father he was up to here
With working on the farm,

pour jars full.

That he was leaving.
Sometimes I wish

Seal while hot.

I had told Olivia, told her either
Where I was going, or told her I wouldn't
Tell her, at times I wish we had

Waited for more money or until

> *Caution: stir daily or else*
> *a foam will appear on top*
> *of the water & the pickles*
> *will be a total loss.*

Spring, when everything rightly
And sweetly begins.

> *Be sure to count the sugar nights.*

II. *Nine Day Pickles*

This is one
Of my favorites.

> *Find a five gallon crock*
> *& use seven pounds*
> *which is six quarts.*

Dale did exactly what
He said he would. He found lots
Of hard work with the railroad,
A gandy-dancer, carrying ties
In that bowlegged gait.

> *Put cucumbers in salt water*
> *heavy enough to float*

Dale also took on extra work
After I knew I was expecting, spent

> *a raw egg. Let stand*
> *three days, drain,*

Winter nights clearing ice
From the bridge trestle cables

put in clear water,
change daily.

And lighting signal lanterns.
He was gone more often
Than not. But he also

Cut in half, cook weak
Vinegar or sour water

Took time for the bottle.
I worried when he drank,
His mood spoiled by night.
I kept myself doctored

with a small lump of tea alum.

And made sure I ate well
And the baby took on
Design, until my body drum rolled.

Cook until water clears,
not more than five minutes.

The rest you find you know:

Heat the following:
Four pounds sugar, vinegar,
a quarter ounce cinnamon bark,

Pushing, bending, breathing

And of course praying. Dale came to see
His son, and I noticed new strength

    & mixed spices (heaped teaspoon).
    Put on pickles hot.
    Boil to seal.

In those well used arms
As he took the child, carried
Like a lantern to the armchair.
He quit drinking that day,
Driving too, though he never
Said why the two went together.

I liked this recipe.
It's good, but takes
so much time.
That was 1929.

    Keep in a crock with plate on top

Times got harder for most after.

    with a stone--scrub stone.

That's what I used.

III. *Bread and Butter Pickles*

    Combine cucumbers & onions

As we got older
Dale and I got along
Less. I remember trying

114

salt & let stand

To grow a garden with that impossible man.
We couldn't agree on
Where to plant or what or when,

> *three hours, drain*
> *Combine seasonings,*

So we grew our own patches,
Only canning together.

> *vinegar & boil.*

The man worked steady and hard,
And that's what took him, finally

> *Heat to simmer. Be careful*
> *to avoid boiling,*

Dying after starting a morning bonfire
Of lumber from the old house.
Now I miss the fighting,
Him burning wagon wheels

> *that ruins them.*
> *Stir real good,*
> *turn fire down,*

I saved to plant flowers around.
I could have argued less,

> *Just so it bubbles.*

But that was what lived
Yet of our passion.

> *Put in a cloth sack.*
> *Be sure you squeeze*
> *all the water.*

In this last decade I've cut
Back, grow less, keep less
From going back,

> *Take both hands, squeeze hard.*

As though Dale had finished all
The hard work, left nothing to me.
Then I quit doing most everything.

No good tomatoes this year.
No sense trying to make relish.

I quit canning.
I even quit canning.

From Emma's Scrapbook: 1935

Daniel Robble has been a minister
for 50 years, so the *Oil City Derrick*
published his picture, a man
with a face like a screen door.

The Reverend *has been present
at 547 weddings and 1109 funerals,*
it says, *and to fill in his time
he has served as Armstrong County
postmaster for 15 years.* He was

the man who solemnized Emma's wedding
to Dale at the Methodist church.
After the ceremony they all went
back to eat at her home-place,
then she and Dale went honeymooning
and—but they cut it short, returning
from Erie when his grandmother died.
Then his family up on Blue Jay Ridge

threw another party. The social
column reported *Those present were
allowed to kiss the bride, but plans
to take the young couple on a merry
old truck ride were not carried out.*
They received 170 presents.

They tried to tie her and Dale
to a hay bale in the back
of a pickup. Dale was having
none of it, and went toe-to-toe
with those who tried. Three men
were at his feet before they

finally gave up. She also recalls
the kisses. She could count them
if she were asked to do so.

From Emma's Scrapbook: 1958

Dale brought home copies
of the Owens-Illinois newsletter
and Emma cut out the article
on him retiring, with a picture
of him in a suit and tie he never
wore to work. He's stretched out
on a chaise lounge his buddies
Leo, Johnnie and Willis bought.
They're in the picture too.

He came home early one day
because his arms had gone numb,
and Doc Ralston said
he'd have to stop working,
that his heart couldn't haul
raw glass in a wheelbarrow
all day. But Emma knew if work
was going to kill him, Dale was
already dead, retired or not.
Emma also knew the chair
would be empty long after
the photograph was taken
and stay that way.

Dale worked for eighteen years
in Plant 17, the article said,
starting in 1941, the young
men all gone overseas. Before,
it says, he worked *in Kane,
Ludlow, Johnsonburg, Renova,
Mahoning and McKees Rocks
at jobs in tanning, mining,
railroading and construction.*

He looks ready, hands on
on the aluminum arms
like they were the handles
of his wheelbarrow, waiting
to get up and get busy
on the next job at hand.

Emma Looks for a Sign

We were planning to go
visit Andy today, then
Will helped his grandson
with the snow on Friday,
and was all played out.
Said he had a headache
and went to bed. I've been
up all night by mistake.
What I meant to say is
I got awake and couldn't
stay in bed. Will's okay,
but I am worried over him
—he gets tired so easy,
and I think it could be
something I don't want
to think about. Yesterday

we had a yard full of robins,
wild geese, and those old
black crows. Will counted
seventy in just one flock.
We had a pair of robins
with snow still falling.
I like seeing the robins.
The others I can take or leave.
I'm looking for the weather

to get good so Will can get better.
When I saw those robins
I licked my thumb and tapped
my fist on my palm, twice,
though once is supposed
to do the trick.

When Will can get things
in the ground he perks
right up. Like to talk him out
of making so much garden,
but when he says:
*Well, the sun's commencing
to get some heat in it,*
I know there's just no
stopping him, if he's able.

From Emma's Scrapbook: 1984

They found an Indian
in Elk County—a body.
The article says he was buried
17 inches below the surface
of a cave floor. Only the bones
are left, with pots and tools
planted by his side.

He had a fractured skull,
and was only 45 years old
when he was laid away,
curled on his side
and covered in bark.

She remembers the Owasco,
her grandmother Myer's people,
a tribe gone for a hundred years.
No hair was left on the body,
but Emma knows it was as dark
as her sister Olivia's,
dark as when the new moon
was coming and you could see
the old one as a slim crescent:

When the new moon is lying
in the old moon's arms,
nothing and no one will
come to harm.

On those nights only that rhyme
could keep Emma sleeping,
knees tucked under her chin,
how the dead man in the cave

was found, the poor man
no one remembers, with a shallow
unmarked grave and a broken head.

Emma on the Darkest Day of the Year

We are going over to my granddaughter's
for Christmas. She sure has a grand
home, but oh my so much work to keep
it clean. White carpets, no less.

My husband Will is a lucky boy, and is
doing real well considering he had two
blood clots on his brain and it took
two doctors a week to figure it out.

It came on sudden. His hair is coming
back real good where they bored in.
I stayed late that night in the hospital,
and if you ask me the nurses weren't

paying him much mind. This is before
they knew what was wrong. They were
going to send him home a vegetable
—I'd have to diaper and bathe him

—then they saw something on a monitor
and before you know it they had him
under and clots pulled out of his head.
When they told me he could die, I was

back in my old kitchen with my first
husband Dale across the table, dying
or dead over breakfast, I'm still not
sure. I was going to let the doctor

know how I feel about it. All it took
was a little look-see, someone paying
attention. I was so mad I could have

just spit. Oh well, this is now.

We sure are having lots of rain, but no
snow, and it's the first day of winter.
I hope it doesn't wait until spring,
then snow when we should be having rain.

I don't go out much. I'm afraid I'll fall.
I fell once, but went down like a feather.
Hope no one spends a lot of money on us.
We don't need anything, now that we're
both home and okay. Just yesterday
Judy took me down to Clarion and I got
a London Fog coat and a two-way dress.
No one needs more than what I got.

Emma Realizes What She Misses

Will is doing real good.
I cut his hair this morning.
It has almost grown in
where they shaved it before
they operated. Didn't do
much else today. Will went
to Clarion with his grandson.
He was gone about one hour
and a half, but I missed him.

My pen takes spells, acts
like it wants to quit.
There, it's going again.
Can't wait until the weather
gets better so I can get out.
It's still rainy and cold.
Will looked out the other day
and said, *We seem to have
an awful lot of rabbits.*
He's worried that they'll
eat our garden when things
come up, and is figuring out
how to get rid of them

—I didn't tell him I fed
them everyday all winter.
They gave me something to do
while he was sick. The snow
was flying and I was tired
of doing nothing. There.
That's the end of that pen.

Emma Does What She Has To

I wanted some plants and flowers out,
so my husband Will worked the ground
and I planted marigolds, lettuce,
broccoli, cauliflower, tomatoes
—something to eat some off.
Will got onion starts out
of the cellar so I put them in.
He was all worn out by then.
His surgery still takes a toll
on him, and I do what he can't.

I do what I can. Will looks better
and eats real good and feels okay.
We are getting by—the insurance
is paying most of his hospital bills.
At least I think it will—I do all
the figuring up and record keeping.

Will was p.o.'d because the doctor
said *no driving*. He sure was mad.
I had to give him a good talking to
so he'd settle down, then we changed
doctors. Dr. Walker said he could
drive one way and I should drive
the other, and I should do any
night driving. Don't like being

behind the wheel, but I didn't say
anything. I'll do what I have to.
I'll do it or get someone to take
us where we need to go. We usually
don't need to go anywhere often.

Emma Aims High

I think every day I will write,
and when the night comes
I sit down and there I sit.
I am so glad to have Will out
of the hospital, though I hardly
got lonesome I was so worried
and busy. He looks good.
We're not getting any more chicks.
Jeff helped Will burn down
the old coop. The fire was white
hot with the all manure going up.
I guess we're done with that.

Back on my old home-place
we never got done working.
Once we had to butcher three hogs
so my father hired a man to kill them
by hitting them between the eyes
with a hammer. But he hit them
again and again and it didn't
take. It was horrible, the squeals,
my father cursing up a storm.
He could never stand for an animal
to suffer. He ran in the house
and got a pistol he used for snakes
and shot the pigs. It's a wonder
he didn't shoot the hired man.

When I married my first husband,
I was surprised he wanted nothing
to do with guns, wouldn't hunt,
even when our son wanted to learn.
Dale said one of his brothers

had been shot up bad.
After Dale died I got a revolver
to keep myself safe. Once, at night,
I heard a noise outside near
the tool shed. I went out
on the porch and fired a shot
that way, into the dark.
It was a bear. I saw him running,
so I shot again, high, to make
sure he would go away.

From Emma's Scrapbook: 1969

Old Annie Bender, *the recluse*
of the Rattlesnake School area
of Cornplanter Township,
the old Seneca reservation,
is dead. She was the midwife
when Emma's first husband was born,
so she must have been very old,
Emma thinks, remembering when
Annie stopped her niece's seizures
with a pouch of herbs, bone,
earth and hair, cured her father
of shingles by throwing hot coals
over his shoulder. Even Emma
went to her, when she had trouble,
and Annie told her to bathe
in rainwater and not to wear
leather. Soon Emma had a son.

But Annie is dead now,
and the paper calls her
a memorable character.
Emma's family always called
her *the old witcher woman,*
but never to her face.

She lived in a stone house
after her wooden one burned.
Annie always blamed the fire
on her enemies. Emma remembers
her as tall, big-shouldered,
until she grew bent, hair
like thistle, always dressed
in full skirts and calf-high

rubber boots. Emma thought
she never looked comfortable.
They told many stories

about Annie, most of them
just that, stories and lies,
and there they were in the paper
for all to see—a whole page
of them which Emma cuts now,
thumbs the creases and spreads
like a map on her kitchen table.

She was the mother of Oklahoma's
Bender Gang is one story. She had
gold buried around her house another.
She carried a knife and flashed it
at people—she was always armed,
Emma knew that much was true.

Other stories Emma could tell:

Annie told time by the sun,
and her mother used to send for her
to prepare the ground for planting.
Annie would take a burning log
from the stove and walk around
the field, swinging the fire
in circles over her head, saying
something Emma does not remember.
The paper also says she used
language not befitting a woman,
but Emma only laughs at that one.

The newspaper describes the day
they found her, near the remains

of a cooking fire in the woods,
her pockets full of leaves
and stems gathered on the cliff
where she had fallen, sycamore
staff snapped in her hand.
At her house they reported
a rickety stove and a scene
of unbelievable squalor.
They found canned food, a straw
tick bed, and a pet rattlesnake.

Christian funeral services
were held April 26. Burial
was in St. Mark's cemetery
near Kossuth in Clarion County.

Emma thinks it's odd how
they stress her being buried
by the church. Emma would
have gone to the service had
she known about it, but somehow
she realizes the ceremony
wasn't important, everyone
who knew Annie knows that.
They do not list survivors,
not even her date of birth,
they only state:
there were no mourners
at the witcher woman's funeral.

Emma Recovers

I have been sick, shook awful
bad, went down to 138 pounds,
but I've gained four back.
I am doing better this week,
another doctor fixed me up.

My husband Will has a good garden
going, which means I'll have to
put it all up in jars and snap
plastic deep freeze containers,
blanching, pickling, making jelly
and sauce. My, that'll be work
—that's what I see when I see
so much growing. Wish I had
a little bit of help sometimes.

I stopped and read this over.
It's sloppy and I had to guess
at half of what I've said.

Now I've gotten busy again,
started some sewing jobs when
I was down. Will and I went
out to the County Market
yesterday and bought
fifty pounds of stew beef
at seventy cents a pound.
You can't beat that.
We went across the road
to his son's for Easter
and got a five pound box
of candy, and lots of good eats.

Will and I also went back down
to Sherritt, near my home-place,
to look up some old friends
like Ella and her husband
Melvin Ruffner. Ella once
was a Foringer, like grandmother,
but I don't think we are
kin, as her people were from

way over in Dubois, but you never
know as we weren't good at keeping
track—there's a whole gaggle
of Foringers at Brady's Bend
what were grandmother's people,
I've never once laid eyes on.
It's good to have lots of family

close. Melvin used to be
a dairy farmer, like Will,
so they hit it right
off and had themselves
quite a time. *Be sure
and come back*, Melvin said.
Ella has been bad all winter.
She had her daughter staying
with her, and they were
quilting together.

From Emma's Scrapbook: 1975

That was some storm for August,
hail slashed down and the ground
was white—it did not look
like snow, Emma thinks, though
that's what people usually say.
The Clarion Democrat publishes
a front page triptych:

There's Harold Bires looking
at his pocked car top,
Ione Mayers with a scooped handful,
like she was displaying diamonds,
and Emma, pulling aside her
black and broken tomato plants
to show the bruised fruit.

You could shovel hailstones
into bushel baskets but she knows
you could never describe the storm
to those who didn't see it.
So Emma saves the page,
even though she looks heavy
in the picture, the dark dress
making her arms look thick,
the plants as chaotic as weeds
she hadn't bothered to pull.
She saves it though she wishes
they had found someone else's ruins,
another garden full of this
sudden harvest of summer ice.

Emma Can See Again

Well, at last I don't have to
go to the doctor for a while.
I am shaky, and if anyone can
read this, they are doing good.

The Lindsay reunion is coming up,
and I hope I can go again.
If I get my new glasses I will
be able to make out who's who.
What a day we had last Friday
—a ton of snow. I could barely
see out my window, even now
without my cataracts.

My husband Will says when I get
around Lindsays I talk up
a storm—good thing nothing's
wrong with my ears, that way
I can hear them back.
Will is doing good
for his eighties, though
he's stone in his right ear
and awful thin. He can't even
hear when I'm in my sewing chair
and he's in his old recliner
—I keep threatening to throw
that thing out in the yard.
I blame his ear on listening
to TV too much, but he says
it's from farm machinery,
and he might have something
there, though I don't let on.

My cataracts are from crocheting,
I suppose, though the eye doctor
says I should keep it up. I never
had trouble with writing though,
my hands knew how to go without me.
I'll bet they'd do the same thing
with my needle and thread.
Tonight I'll try crocheting
without looking at my lap.
Wouldn't that be something
if it really worked?

Emma's First Husband's Brothers and Sisters

Dale had a bunch of kin.
His father had two wives
in a row, and two big families,
but they were all strange,
mostly. There was Katherine,
Everett, Noah, Guy, Edward
and Julia in the first family.
There was Jessie, Rebecca, Harry,
Elizabeth, Minnie, Thomas, Alice,
Mary, Ellen and Dale in the second.

Eddie, Katherine and Everett
died as babies.

Noah lived alone all his life
in a shack on Blue Jay Ridge.
They say he was so ignorant
he couldn't count past ten.
At the grocery store he'd pay
for one item at a time
so he'd know he wasn't cheated
when they added it all up.

Guy worked as a cable car conductor
in Erie and was killed in a brawl.
All the Lindseys were hot-headed.

Jessie died at two months.
Rebecca and Ellen were stillborn.

The girls in this family

were as normal as any Lindsay.
Elizabeth, Mary and Minnie
all married and had kids,
and all are dead now.
The only one left is Alice,
and she took a trip around
the bend. She's a nurse,
and all kinds of crazy
about things being clean.
Never had any children
that I know of.

Thomas was killed in car accident.

Harry lived on Blue Jay Ridge
in an old aluminum pull trailer.
He was the one what liked reading,
and went out west once
to cowboy. Came back
alive but with a few slugs
in him for his trouble.
He's dead too. Paid for
his funeral thirty years
before, even bought a suit
at the second-hand store
in Clarion to be buried in.
Said it was *Good enough to rot.*
A Lindsay never walked
what would waste a bent nail.

Dale married me. I think I got
the one sane one of the whole
Lindsay clan. What was a body
to do with the rest of them?

From Emma's Scrapbook: 1988

A PEEK AT THE PAST

Not many area residents recall
the way Market Street, Kittaning,
looked in 1910, when people used
horses and buggies and the trolley.

Emma does. She remembers going
to town and riding up Market
in her father's wagon, her mother
perched up on the front seat
with him, she and Olivia
sitting as primly as they could
on a crate in the back.

That was one of the first times
she saw her first husband, Dale.
He was standing on the steps
of the sundry, an older boy
holding the reins of a team,
his father inside the store,
looking worn from working
on their mountain farm, a clench
already possessed his jaw.
She knew him from a barn-raising,
maybe, or was it a church supper,
then her mother, spying her
looking his way, said:

That's one of those Lindsays
from up on Blue Jay Ridge.
Pay him no never mind. Those
Scots-Irish are a hard lot.

Now Emma is not sure
if she should have minded her,
but by then she had traded
a glance with him, and knew
he'd remember her when
she saw him in the future.

From Emma's Scrapbook: 1990

When Emma sees the article
on Reye's Syndrome and aspirin
she saves it, understanding
very little of what it says.
But she thinks of her baby
brother Freddie teething,
and the old witcher woman
giving him willow branches
to chew. The article says

aspirin was found in willow.
She remembers how deeply
Freddie slept all day,
how he'd be up all night,
crying until the dawn racket
of birds distracted him,
that and the growing light.

Now they say the willow bark
might have made him hard
to wake. Now they say it,
Emma thinks, though she knows
they would have never doubted
Annie Bender, she who saved
her mother in breach birth,
had told Emma what to do when
the change came on her.
Emma chewed the branch too,
drank Annie's teas, wore
her poultices and pouches,
and now she finds herself
sleepier than ever before.

Emma Watches Other People Work

August 1

I am feeling pretty good
but not like I like to be.
I want to get my cleaning
lady started this week.
Will got a new go-by-itself
lawnmower and is now taking
weeds out of the rhubarb.
His grandson Jeff has a nice
big dog, but he chases cars.
When he comes over here
I go out and send him home
in a hurry. It's a good time
to fish, but I wasn't down
to the ponds all last year.
Will caught one 19 incher,
the others were smaller.

August 3

I have a lady cleaning house
for me. She does real good
at four dollars an hour.
I used to get fifty cents
a day, two-fifty a week.
Oh well, then and today
are different. Glad for that.

Will is reading up on his mower.
Can't wait for him to go outside
so I can sit and make a rug
without him bothering me about

how low it cuts, about the fish
he caught, a catfish, 19 inch,
and a few smaller. If he thinks
he can talk me into going down
to the ponds and fish, he's got
another thing coming. He didn't
fish much when I wasn't good.
He stayed in the house with me.

I can't get a rag rug done
without some old clothes.
Need jeans and shirts, no towels
or underclothes, but I have
trouble getting people to save
for me. I am feeling good
but keeping my fingers crossed.

August 5

What a hot day. I am pretty
shaky today for no good
reason. The water is running off
my face right now. I am sitting
here at the kitchen table
in my nightgown. It is nine
in the morning and it's going
to have to cool down some if
I'm to get any baking done.

August 6

Will and the cleaning lady
and I put up 52 quarts of peaches
yesterday and today. I sterilized
the jars. Will is listening

to the radio ballgame and seeing
it at the same time on TV.
The Pirates are ahead, he said,
as if I'd bother writing that down.
The radio has too much static in it
for me to listen—must be storming
somewhere. I am all done in—all
the work this week tired me out.

Emma Tires

It seems I get tired easy,
and am ready for bed.
I just wear out and can't
do any more. There, I said
that enough times, went
over that more than once.

My husband Will cooks
and can do everything
when I can't. He loves
TV and has it on right now,
but I can't bear to watch it
—don't know why. I don't
have many flowers, but
am waiting for spring all
the same. I don't crochet
anymore as it hurts my eyes.
I don't bake or anything.
Will has to eat store bread.
I feel bad as he's never
had to do that in his life.

It is awfully muddy here,
a sloppy winter. I have
one geranium in bloom
—I'll put it out later
when it warms up some.
It's a purple one. I look
at it for a long time, never
get tired of looking at it.

From Emma's Scrapbook: 1991

The *Oil City Derrick* has a story
about Mick Moyta who has worked
for the last 83 years, a shoemaker.
It tells his whole life story.
He was a Russian prisoner from
the Austria-Hungarian army
where he learned to fix boots
for Ukrainian guards—much more
complicated than Emma can
keep straight. Live long enough,
she thinks, and anyone has
a story to tell. She remembers

taking Andy there the day
before school for new soles
on his shoes as he always
walked on the inside
of his heels and wore them down.
Moyta would tell him a good
soldier would not march
his shoes off and her son
would try to walk straighter.

Moyta says that he has few
customers now, that only one
mother brought a pair of shoes
to fix after the summer.
He is 98 years old and Emma
wonders how he keeps going.
She knows he must have
his share of aches and pains.

Emma Stays in the House

January

My husband Will sits and sleeps.
The weather is awful cold,
so we don't go out, only
for the mail. I haven't been
good lately. I guess
I am what they call *housebound*.

March

I am slow at writing.
Will went down to the ponds
to see how the fish made it
through the winter—he saw
bass. At first I felt
rough today, but I think
it will work out. At least
I can do as I please, even
if I have trouble walking.

April

Will wants to make garden.
I have to sit him down
and talk to him a lot
—he'd overdo it if I didn't.
He'll not be doing anything
if the rain doesn't quit.
That's all they're calling for
this week. Today Will walked
down to the ponds but didn't see
any fish. The water is all

black as the Amish are plowing
and it all runs right in.

May

We are having pretty weather.
I'm not doing much, just can't.
A new lady's been coming in
to clean, but I'm not sure
she'll work out. I did away
with most of my flowers, even
the begonias I wintered over
for years. They were mostly
exhausted anyhow. Will does
some yard work. He made

a little garden—tomatoes
and onions. At least he is
doing some better. He gets
around, and gained some weight.

July

Will's onions didn't get a bit
nice, just rotted in the ground.
Hardly any tomato blossoms.
I go to bed thinking about
my family, then get up before
long and write about them.

Will mows a little, does a few
things. I don't get around
very good anymore.

September

We put up six quarts of tomatoes
this fall. We didn't make much
garden. Had no flowers. Neither
of us was able. The doctor says
we're both doing okay, but I worry
about Will. I'd sure be lonesome
without him. I'm not even sure
I would be able to get along.

December

We weren't out to my son
Andy's for Christmas. I can't
take the riding. I haven't been
good for as long as I can
remember. We have both been
out-of-order. The nurse
is coming in to see Will.
Didn't see anyone over
the holidays. We had good
eats brought right to us
by the Meals on Wheels.
Will sits and eats everything
they bring, but I just pick
around. He's been in and out
of the hospital twice this month.

I sent out the coins I saved
over the year to my great grandson
for Christmas, and they say he sat
quietly and counted it all up.
I always thought it best when
little boys were kept busy.

I am in the kitchen now,
and it is getting colder.
If it gets much worse
I'll have to go to bed
just to get warm, even
though I'm not sleepy
and have more I'd like
to get down. But I'll
be stuck there. Seems
all I ever do is rest.

Emma to Herself

The words are in odd shapes.
I guess I am not in the mood
to write. But here goes.

The boys who work these farms,
ours and the one across the way,
did not get the corn picked,
and it all turned black.
Will was out and picked
three pails for the birds
right after first frost.

Then it all darkened.
My, what a loss that will be.

My son's face aches.
Hasn't been to visit,
haven't seen them
since the harvest.
We call and they call.
We would like to go out there
but I don't think he feels
like having company.

We just heard a shot,
and when we looked we saw
two Amish fleeing
in their blue and black clothes.
They shoot their deer anytime
they like, but what I can't figure

is they know winter brings the fat
thick, the hide dark, the meat strong.

The lane they use is rutted and washed,
and the women seem as tired
as when I worked like I used to.

Emma: Epilogue at 94

Hip broken, Emma rises after surgery
with a last breath to ask
her son Andy if he is still married
to the same woman.

Yes, mother, he answers. *For fifty years.*
He wonders how she could forget.

I'm looking for another, she says.
She lays back down and adds, *I've had two
husbands, but men don't seem to last.*

Naton Leslie is the author of a book of narrative nonfiction, *That Might Be Useful* (Lyon Press, 2005), and five volumes of poetry: *Three Shadows Are Dark Daughters* (1998), *Moving to Find Work* (2000), *Salvaged Maxims* (2002), *Egress* (2004), and *The Last Best Motif* (2004). A collection of his short fiction, *Marconi's Dream and Other Stories* (2003), won the George Garrett Fiction Prize, and he is the recipient of fellowships from the National Endowment for the Arts and the New York Foundation for the Arts. He teaches writing and literature at Siena College, in Loudonville, New York. He lives in Ballston Spa, New York, with his wife Susan and their family.